# THE TIME OF THE KACHINAS

BY
BARBARA WINTHER

Pen and ink drawings by Barbara Winther,
water colored by Lynn Cooper

OLD BEAR PUBLISHING

ISBN: 1497555388
ISBN 13: 9781497555389

Dedicated to our good Hopi friends,
the Lomayaktewa family.

# TABLE OF CONTENTS

Preface · · · ix

The First Kachina · · · 1

Coyote's Dance · · · 7

Warrior Field Mouse · · · 13

Planting The Pahos · · · 19

Buffalo Dance · · · 25

A Visit From Two Kachinas · · · 31

Ogre Woman · · · 39

Nataskas · · · 45

The Great Procession · · · 53

Clan Race · · · · · · · · · · 63

Corn Dance · · · · · · · · · · 67

Butterfly Dance · · · · · · · · · · 77

The Kachinas Go Home · · · · · · · · · · 83

Glossary · · · · · · · · · · 89

Kachina Images in Book · · · · · · · · · · 95

Non-Kachina Images in Book · · · · · · · · · · 96

Acknowledgments · · · · · · · · · · 97

## MAP OF THE SOUTHWEST UNITED STATES

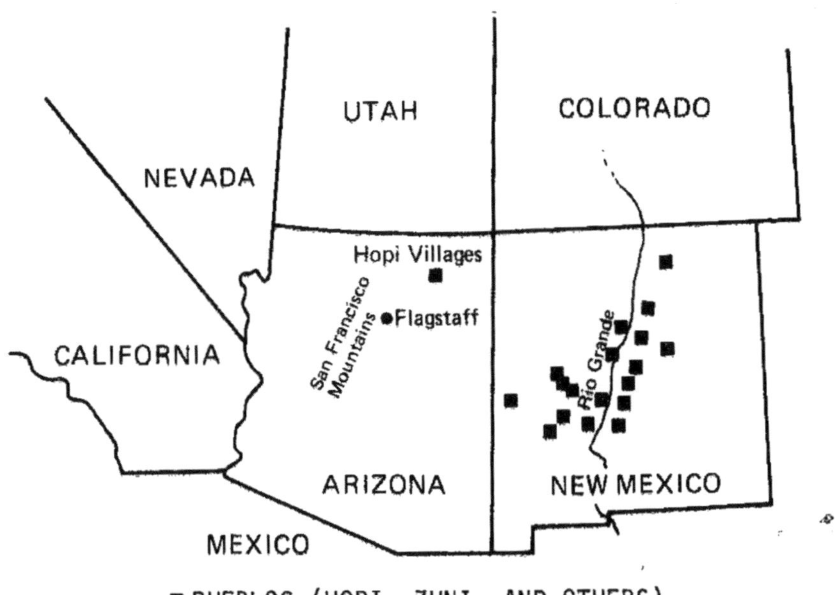


■ PUEBLOS (HOPI, ZUNI, AND OTHERS)

## MAP OF THE HOPI MESAS

# PREFACE

For over a thousand years, the Hopi people have lived in villages near or on top of three mesas in the arid plateau region of what today is called northeastern Arizona. To the Hopi, their survival in this bleak desert land depends on the Kachinas (*Katsinas*)—messenger spirits who for the most part embody the forces of nature, mainly those related to rain.

The stories in this book are about a fictional Hopi family who live in one of the mesa villages on the Hopi Reservation. Through the eyes of Hester, nine, and Honu, seven, you learn about yearly events that occur during the time of the Kachinas. Although these events are an accurate, historical compilation, they do not occur in all Hopi villages and, when they do, often they are performed in different ways by Kachinas who vary in how they look.

Barbara Winther, 2014

TIME: LATE NOVEMBER, BEFORE SOYAL (SOLSTICE).

# THE FIRST KACHINA

Although the sun shone brightly, by early afternoon it was still cold. Breath clouds formed in front of faces and frosty ground crunched under feet like glass beads. The air smelled of burning juniper. Now and then, when a doorway opened, the odor of newly made bread and lamb stew drifted out.

Around the main plaza, villagers gathered, some standing on rooftops, others grouped in front of houses. Two elders sat on the stone bench. Most of the young children stood close to their parents. Women and girls were wrapped in shawls or blankets while men and boys were bare-armed and appeared not to notice the cold. Voices remained subdued. Even the dogs were quiet; they sniffed the air and padded around as if bent on important business.

Hester, nine, and her brother Honu, seven, stood between Mother and Father in front of Aunt Laura's house. Nearby, Grandmother, eyes closed, leaned on her cane. Three older cousins had climbed onto the rooftop.

The tips of Hester's fingers felt numb and her toes seemed to be turning into icicles. She glanced nervously at Mother then at Father then at her feet. I won't freeze, she told herself and clenched her teeth so they would stop chattering.

She wiped her runny nose on her sleeve and stared at the top of a ladder just beyond the plaza. It rose from an opening in the ground and jutted up skeleton-like against the sky.

Hester knew the ladder led underground to what her father called a *kiva*. She had no idea what a *kiva* looked like. Or what happened inside. Those were secrets she wasn't supposed to know. However, she couldn't help wondering if today Grandfather was down there. Her older brother, William, too. And Uncle Ramon. She hadn't seen them all morning. Did they have something to do with what was supposed to happen?

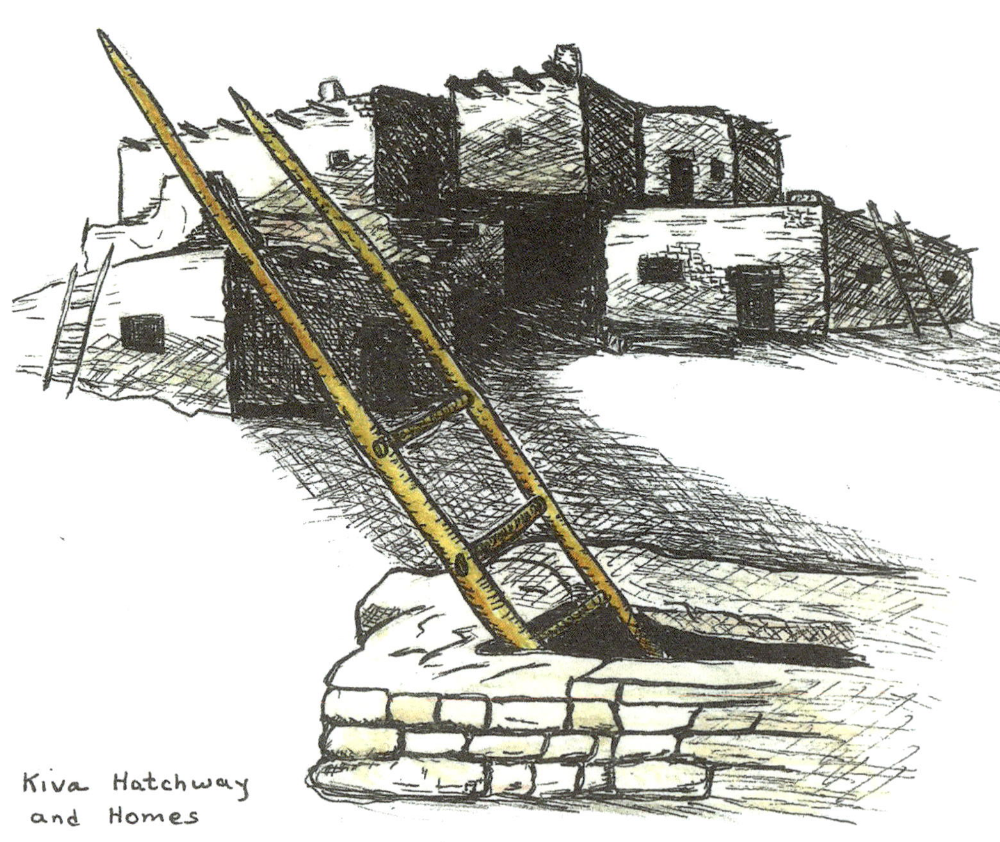

Kiva Hatchway and Homes

Last week Grandfather had said, "Hester, you are only nine years old. Soon the time will come when you will learn about these things. Until then, do not ask."

So she continued to look and wait, rubbing her hands together, wiggling her toes, wiping her nose on her sleeve, clenching her teeth, and saying nothing.

A hush spread over the people. Eyes focused on the path to the southeast, the one that led up to the mesa. A jingling of bells floated on the air. Hester caught her breath. That must be *Soyal.* The Kachina is coming. He's coming.

She knew what he looked like. He had visited the village this time last year and the year before, her memory vague before that. She leaned forward as a figure appeared. Ah, yes, *Soyal.* Fascinated, she watched the figure with the blue-green head slowly enter the village. He wore in an old, white hunting shirt, ceremonial kilt and sash. A turtle shell clip-clopped behind his right knee. A gourd rattle whispered in his right hand. In his other hand he carried feathered sticks and a pouch.

*Soyal* staggered.

Villagers raised their hands as if to steady him. *Soyal* began to dance in an awkward manner as if he had forgotten the steps. A ripple of laughter swept through the spectators. Hester remembered this from last year. Still it seemed wrong to laugh at a Kachina. But he did act kind of funny. Did he want us to laugh?

Father leaned down and said softly to Hester and Honu, "*Soyal Kachina* travels a long way. He is as old as time but as new as a sprout from a seed. Each year he visits to help life start again. He wants us to know the trip has been hard."

At a home near the plaza *Soyal* stopped. Taking corn meal from his pouch he traced four horizontal lines on the wall next to the door. He moved to the Flute *Kiva* and stopped to sing a song so low the words could

Soyal
Kachina

not be heard. On to the plaza he staggered. There he performed a shaky dance, gasping and breathing heavily. Next he moved to the *kiva* near the plaza. He planted his four feathered sticks near the hatchway, sprinkled corn meal and shook his gourd rattle twice.

A head appeared from the darkness below.

As the figure climbed up the *kiva* ladder to give the blessing, Honu grinned at Mother and announced, "That's Grandfather."

Mother's look told him to be still.

After a short ceremony, *Soyal* stumbled off to the *Powamu Kiva.* There, a similar ceremony took place. Then he left, walking down the path he had used to enter the village. Hester wanted to ask where he was going but knew she would get no answer. She closed her eyes and strained her ears, listening to the tinkle of bells until she heard them no more.

People started back to their homes. As they went, they exchanged greetings and smiled. Sounds of laughter erupted, feet crunched on the frozen earth, doors opened and closed; a burro brayed, a rooster crowed, a dog barked.

Hester stared at the *kiva* where she had seen Grandfather. The empty ladder rose tall against the brilliant blue sky. She knew the ceremony had been important. And she knew from the years before that it was only after *Soyal* came that other Kachinas visited the village. Now begins the time of the Kachinas, she said to herself. Taking Honu's hand, she walked home behind Mother and Father. She no longer felt the cold.

TIME: DECEMBER, DURING THE DANGEROUS MOON.

# COYOTE'S DANCE

Cold air seeped through tiny cracks and spread its fingers into the corners of the house. Little Honu pushed closer to the iron stove. He continued to tell himself, I'm hot, I'm hot, in hopes thinking would make it true.

Mother would not return until morning. She had gone to Aunt Laura's house to help bring a baby into the world. Grandmother, eyes closed, sat on her sheepskin by the stove, her head and shoulders wrapped in a wool shawl. Hester, Honu's older sister, huddled at Grandmother's feet.

As Honu inched toward the heat, he glanced at the stack of dry, twisted juniper limbs and then looked up at his father. He hoped it was enough to last the night. Although the idea of going outside to get more wood sent shivers through his body, he never would admit he was cold to anyone. "Hopi men do not feel the cold," Grandfather had said.

Father opened the stove door and shoved in another stick, then returned to sit on his stool.

"Are the Kachinas cold?" Honu asked.

Father smiled. "They don't feel the weather. They bring it."

"Where are they now? What are they doing? Why are they making it so cold?"

"That"—Father's voice was stern—"is not for a little boy to know."

"How come?"

"That is the way it is."

The fire cracked like a whip. Honu jumped. A gust whooed in under the door. He swallowed hard and moved closer to the fire.

Grandmother stirred and blinked like an owl. "At this time of year we must all be careful." Her voice sounded mixed with gravel. "I never do important things in December, especially at night."

"Yes," said Father, "what Grandmother says is important to remember. These nights are only good for telling stories."

"Then, tell us one," Honu insisted, dancing in place to get his feet warm. "I'm tired of having nothing to do."

"How can Father tell us anything," Hester said, "if you keep talking and jumping around."

Honu frowned. He wished his sister was younger and made more mistakes.

"*Haliksai,*" said Father.

This was the way he always started a story. It was a signal for everyone to listen. Honu plopped down onto his sheepskin. Father cleared his throat and began

Coyote and his wife lived at Ishmovala. Now you know how nosey Coyote is. He prowls about and sniffs at things. Long ago he used to slink around to watch the Kachinas dance. He saw Red-tailed Hawk dance. He went north of Squash Seed Point and watched *Hototo.*

Then he crept over to Katsinvala, where many Kachinas live, and poked around there for a long time.

Being a jealous, greedy animal, Coyote wanted to be like these Kachinas. He wanted their power. So one morning he called a meeting of his coyote friends. For miles around they came, some from as far off as the Grand Canyon.

Hototo
2nd Mesa

When they all were seated in his *kiva*, Coyote announced, "We shall perform a Kachina dance. Each of you find skin and cloth, feathers and yarn, old gourds and shells, and anything else you think would be interesting to wear. Two days from now, dress up and come back. Then, while I smoke a pipe down in my *kiva*, all of you dance in front of the juniper tree that grows from the large rock. My wife will sit in the shade of the tree and watch you perform. In this way we shall all become powerful spirits."

Now it happened that Oraibi village had a coyote hunt on the day of Coyote's dance at Ishmovala. The people were tired of having their lambs stolen. Some men ran north. Others ran south. They spread out and formed a circle, then began moving back towards Oraibi. As they walked, they shouted and beat the bushes. To their surprise, no coyotes. But when they reached Ishmovala, they heard yelping, thumping and rattling.

Up from a hole in the ground rose a strange line of creatures, broken feathers on their heads, yarn over their eyes. They wore ragged kilts and straggly sashes. They didn't know how to dance. They stamped on all four feet, their rattles between their teeth.

One of the younger men suggested they might be ogres. A village elder thought they were witches. As the men drew closer, they realized they were only coyotes.

The men circled the group. At a signal they advanced, shouting and waving their sticks. The terrified coyotes ran this way and that. They yipped and yapped, trying to escape. So much yarn covered their eyes that they couldn't see and their sashes were so droopy that they stumbled over them.

During this confusion, Coyote's wife hid behind the juniper rock and Coyote peeked out of his *kiva* and realized he was safer below. He put out his pipe and waited until the sun set and no more sounds were above him.

After their successful hunt, the men returned to Oraibi. They told their families about the silly coyotes that tried to be Kachinas. They laughed and laughed except for one elder who didn't think it funny.

He shook his head. "Better look out when you walk across the desert," he said. "Kachinas can get upset by crazy business."

As for Coyote and his wife, they finally came out of hiding and sneaked away. To this day, when the full moon rises they climb to the top of Coyote Ridge, tip their noses into the air, and cry. Not about the loss of their coyote friends. No, they are far too selfish to care about what happens to anyone else. Instead, they cry because they have no Kachina power.

Father leaned back. For a while, the only sounds were from the crackling fire and the swooshing wind. At last he said, "That's the end of the story."

Honu snickered. "I bet the Kachinas thought the coyotes were funny to dance around like that."

"I don't think so," said Father. "It was a bad idea."

"Well, yesterday I pretended I was Eagle Kachina." Honu raised his arms. "I swooped around and did a wild dance."

"I know."

"How?"

"I was told."

Honu lowered his arms and glared at Hester, but she shook her head. Then he remembered she hadn't been around. Who could have seen him? "Was that a wrong thing to do?" he asked.

His father replied, "That, too, was a bad idea."

Honu swallowed hard and hoped the Kachina would forgive him.

Grandmother said, "You should dance like Warrior Field Mouse." She laughed with a raspy wheeze.

"Yes, like Warrior Field Mouse," Father said. "An excellent idea."

"How did he dance?"

Father smiled. "I was about your age when I first heard the story. It is time you heard it. "*Haliksai,*" said Father and he began the story.

Eagle

TIME: DECEMBER, DURING THE DANGEROUS MOON.

# WARRIOR FIELD MOUSE

Once there was a village with many chickens. The people took good care of them and the chickens laid many eggs. Then one day a villager discovered the feathers and bones of two chickens in the middle of the plaza. The next day, someone else found more feathers and bones. People were alarmed. They took turns keeping a careful watch until they discovered the killer. It was a large hawk that lived on a rock north of the village.

All day the women talked about what the men should do. All night the men considered what the women had talked about. The children thought up many plans. But nobody did anything to get rid of the hawk. On the following day, two more chickens were gone.

On the east side of the village lived Field Mouse. When he heard about the trouble, he felt sorry for the people. He scampered over to the Village Chief and said, "I'll kill the hawk."

"You!" exclaimed the Chief. "How can a tiny mouse kill a strong, swift hawk when even we villagers don't know how."

"I can do it," insisted Field Mouse. "Tell the Crier Chief to make the announcement. Your enemy will be gone in four days."

"The Village Chief tried not to show his amusement, for he was impressed by the small animal's determination. The next morning the Crier climbed to the housetop and called out the news. The people couldn't believe their ears. At first they laughed. Then they were upset. "A mouse cannot do what we cannot," they said.

Three days later, Field Mouse hunted until he found a long, strong stick. He dragged it down into his hole and sharpened one end to a fine point. To the east he dug a tunnel and then burrowed upwards, coming to the surface with a tiny opening quite a distance from his hatchway. That night when the stars were right, Field Mouse attached eagle feathers to his head. He painted white clay on his face and body and dressed himself, making certain his ceremonial kilt was clean and his sash correctly tied. Across each shoulder he draped a bandolier. Feeling the warrior spirit, he picked up his bow and war club. With great focus and determination, he sat down to plan his dance and compose his song. All night long he practiced down in his kiva.

Meanwhile, although the village people didn't believe the mouse had a chance, for three days they did their part to help. The women and girls ground corn and made *piki.* The men butchered sheep and carried water up from the springs. And the boys brought wood for the fires. As the fourth day dawned, the people washed their heads in yucca suds and dressed in their best clothes as they always did for an important event.

At noon Field Mouse climbed out of his hole. He faced the north and began to dance and sing, keeping close to his hatchway.

"Though Hawk kills chickens,
He can't kill me.
Nothing can catch
Fast little Field Mouse."

Warrior
Mouse

Over and over he sang his song and danced. The villagers thought this was pretty funny but they didn't dare laugh although a few girls giggled.

Killer Hawk, watching from the rock, wasn't amused. He saw Field Mouse as a tasty meal. With a screech he flew down to capture the little creature.

"Run, Field Mouse," cried the people. "Run, run."

Field Mouse ducked into his hole.

Killer Hawk flew back to the rock. Ruffling his feathers in disgust, he glared down.

Field Mouse again came out to dance and sing, this time to the west and further out from his hatchway.

"Though hawk kills chickens,

He can't kill me.

Nothing can catch

Fast little Field Mouse."

With a louder screech, Killer Hawk swooped down.

The people gasped and shouted, "Run, Field Mouse, run."

Field Mouse scurried for his hole, reaching safety just in time.

Killer Hawk shook his wings indignantly, then flew back to the rock where he sat, clicking his beak in anger.

Again Field Mouse came out to dance and sing, this time to the south and even further away from his hatchway.

"Though hawk kills chickens,

He can't kill me.

Nothing can catch

Fast little Field Mouse."

An old grandfather whispered, "Field Mouse dances too far from safety." Down sped screaming Killer Hawk, talons outstretched.

"Run, run," shouted the people.

Away dashed Field Mouse. He reached his hole within a whisker of being caught. At the bottom of his ladder he paused, breathing heavily, scared but determined to carry out his plan. He carried his sharp stick along the tunnel and pushed it up through the tiny opening he had dug—it was a long way from his hatchway.

For the fourth time Field Mouse courageously ventured out, dancing and singing, this time to the east. He pranced further and further away from his hatchway, closer and closer to the tiny opening.

"Go back," cried the people. "You have danced too far."

But Field Mouse continued to dance and sing, showing no sign of fear.

"Though hawk kills chickens,
He can't kill me.
Nothing can catch
Fast little Field Mouse."

For more emphasis, Field Mouse stopped beside his tiny opening, gave a squeaky war cry and shook his club.

This made Killer Hawk so mad he trembled. Straight for the mouse he zoomed, talons clawing the air, ready to sink into flesh.

"Run," screamed the people. But Field Mouse stood his ground. At the last second he slipped into the tiny opening and firmly held onto the stick. The hawk landed directly on the sharp point and died. Shouts rang from the villagers. "Killer Hawk is gone. Our chickens are saved. Field Mouse is a great warrior.

Father leaned forward, opened the stove door and shot another piece of wood into the fire. He said, "In honor of the brave little mouse, a feast was held. Even today we remember the courage of the clever, little creature that faced the strong, swift enemy.

Honu sat still, his eyes large and bright.

Hester crept closer to the fire.

Except for the occasional popping of an ember, it was silent inside the house. Outside, an eerie wind whistled as if trying to find a way inside.

"Well," said Father, "enough story-telling for tonight."

"I shall be brave and clever," Honu announced. "You'll see. I shall be like Warrior Field Mouse."

Father stood up and stretched his arms. "I hope so."

A sudden series of snorts and shushes drowned out the wind.

"Grandmother is snoring," said Hester, smothering a giggle.

"Ah," said Father, "she's telling her own story. She has heard mine too many times."

TIME: LATE DECEMBER, AT THE END OF SOYAL.

# PLANTING THE PAHOS

Early one morning, when the sky was still completely black, Mother called to Hester, "Time to get up and wash your hair. Then it will be dry by dawn."

Hester remembered this was the morning to plant *pahos*, prayer feathers. In the afternoon the funny *Kököle Kachinas* would come to dance in the plaza and give out presents. She hoped they would play games with the children as they had last year.

Blinking to drive out sleep, she nudged Honu on the mat beside her. "Wake up, little brother, wake up."

"No," Honu muttered, snuggling under the blanket and hoping he would be forgotten.

Father, who was building a fire in the stove, said to Uncle Ramon, "Honu isn't a Hopi after all."

"I guess not," said the uncle. "Hopi men know how to jump out of sleep. They don't feel the cold."

"I am too Hopi," Honu cried, crawling from his warmth. With a shudder, he reached for his long-sleeved shirt. "It's not cold at all."

"Good," said the uncle. "Then you can help."

"Doing what?"

KöKöle

"We need you to run naked to Grandmother's peach trees. There you can plant *pahos* so the trees will bear good fruit."

Honu pressed his lips together and tried not to shiver. "Yes, that is what I can do," he said in a small voice, although he wanted to crawl back under the covers instead. After all it was still dark outside. He could get a little more warmth in his bed. But nobody else was under the covers. Even his sister Hester was up, washing her hair in yucca suds. He sighed, took off his shirt, and scrambled to his feet. "I am warm and ready to run," he announced. Even so, he moved close to the fire.

Just before dawn, Hester, her hair still damp, peeked out the window and saw messengers wearing feathered wreaths come out of *kivas* to deliver the prayer feathers to each family. William, her older brother, was the *kiva* messenger to their house. Mother received the feathered sticks, and the family listened carefully as he explained what prayer must be made with each kind of *pahos*. He held out a group. "These are prayers for the sun. Plant them carefully so our crops will grow well. The owl-feathered *pahos* are for the peach trees. These will help the corn and squash grow. And plant these at the springs, so water may always be there. Each of you has a prayer here. This one is for the house—for health and happiness."

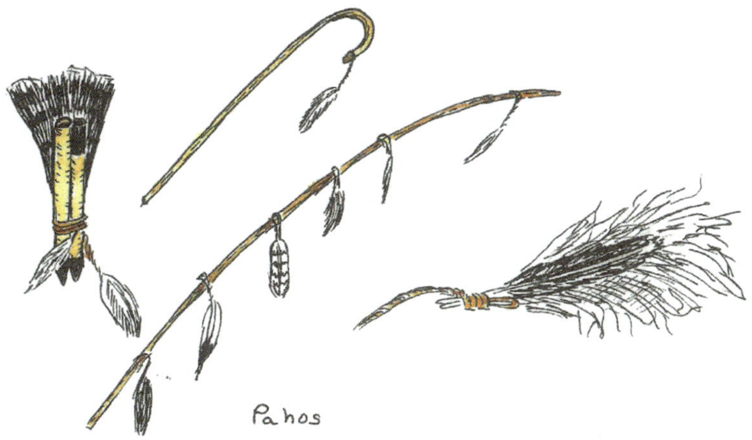

Carrying bundles of *pahos*, Hester followed Mother and Grandmother outside. All of the women and girls of the village were walking eastward, carrying their bundles. At the shrine near the edge of the mesa, the people met and planted the feathered sticks firmly in the ground. They drew paths to the east by trickling a fine line of cornmeal from their fingers. Then they stood, wrapped in their shawls, praying silently, waiting for the sun to rise.

Hester watched the sky turn yellow and pink. Shapes took form on the desert below the mesa. It always surprised her how small everything looked down there. The bare branches of the cottonwood trees near the wash reminded her of a row of prayer feathers. Beyond, Grandmother's peach trees looked like tufts of eagle down.

The wide, flat-topped mountain of another mesa was sharply drawn against the sky. She loved to travel there with her family, especially when they went for social dances.

She looked to the southwest and could barely see the tall, snowy mountains where the Kachinas lived. Suddenly, their peaks glowed red as if on fire. A sign from the Kachinas, she thought, awed by the sight. They must know we are thinking about them.

The sun began its journey across the sky. A breath of wind touched Hester's face. She closed her eyes and prayed along with the others for all to be blessed in the Hopi Way.

At dawn Father gave Honu a bundle of green-sticked *pahos*, each with an owl feather dangling from a cotton string. "Plant some under the peach trees," he said. "Tie others to the branches. Run all the way there to make your prayers strong."

Honu watched Father and Uncle Ramon race off toward Antelope Shrine with their feathered sticks. He saw other men meet them, also running naked, a sign of purity and strength. All carried prayer sticks. Some carried bells. Shouts of "Ah-hoo!" and silver tinkling carried far in the crisp, still air.

Turning in the opposite direction, Honu ran to the edge of the mesa. Below, two other boys were running down the steep path. As Honu rushed down the same way, he shouted to the sky, "This is easy, easy, easy."

Out across the desert he ran, breathing harder, his skin glowing and tingling. He was excited and proud to be running with the prayer feathers. Twice he leaped over bushes. Once he startled a rabbit. It jumped in the air and dashed away. "This is easy, easy, easy," Honu cried, running faster.

Honu ran for a long time. Yet the peach trees still looked far away. Although he had lost the cold, running was getting harder. Not enough breath for his lungs.

I cannot make it, he thought, alarm shooting tiny arrows all over his body. The ground tried to hold onto his feet. A dull ache grew in his chest. I will fall over and pass out. I will die. Tomorrow they will find my skeleton picked clean by eagles. Mother and Father will cry. Everyone will say poor Honu should have stayed home under the covers.

He thought it might be an excellent idea to drop his prayer feathers, lie down, and take a nap in the sun. After all, the other boys had disappeared. Nobody would know. He could rest and gain strength. Then, pick up the feathers and continue.

A lump grew in his throat. He remembered the time William found him asleep instead of guarding the sheep. How embarrassed Honu had been. "A coyote might have carried off a lamb," his brother had said, "or the flock could have strayed."

From far off, Honu heard the tinkling of bells and the faint shouts of "Ah-hoo!" The men were still running to Antelope Shrine. He swallowed the lump away. I have a duty, he told himself. For the good of my family, I must do it.

The lump came back and he swallowed again. I will not sleep in the sun, he informed himself. Besides, the Kachinas might find out. They would think me weak and I am not. I am strong. I will not die. I will not take a nap. I will keep on running. I will plant strong prayers.

"Ah-hoo!" he called out painfully.

A surprising energy flowed through his body.

"Ah-hoo!" he shouted again.

His breath came easier, his chest felt better and his legs gained strength.

The peach trees drew closer. A smile filled Honu's face. He knew he could bring the prayers to Grandmother's trees.

"Ah-hoo! Ah-hoo!"

When Honu came back to the house, Father tied a prayer feather in his hair and said, "May you always make the right decision."

Hester whispered, "He is proud of you."

From a housetop the Crier Chief called, "Tomorrow rabbit hunting will start. On the fourth day there will be a feast."

Later that morning, Grandfather arrived for mutton stew, *piki* bread, and corn pudding, his first time eating at home since the start of *Soyal.*

TIME: MID JANUARY, DURING PAMUYA, WHEN THE MOON APPEARS TO MOVE NORTH AGAIN.

# BUFFALO DANCE

Since the beginning of the January moon there had been night dances in the *kivas*. During the days, men often strode back and forth on the frozen streets, their shirts bulging with hidden objects. In the late afternoons, sounds of singing, stamping, and rattling rose from the hatchways. Children stopped to listen.

On some nights, adults went to the *kivas*, the children left at home. The same muffled sounds of late afternoons rose into the darkness; children dreamed of the time when they, too, could attend night dances.

"Are Kachinas in the *kivas* now?" Honu asked one afternoon as he came into the house.

Mother stirred the cornmeal mush on the stove. "Don't ask about such things," she replied. "Maybe next year you and Hester will be initiated. Until then, do not make the Kachinas angry by asking about them."

The front door opened. It was Aunt Laura. She peered down at Honu. "Why do you look so sad?" she asked.

"I am tired of being a little boy."

"But you are growing up quickly." She rolled her eyes and ruffled his hair. "Handsome, too. It will be a lucky woman who finds you for a husband. She may catch you today."

"Today!" exclaimed Honu in horror. "I'm not ready to be a husband."

"Here," said Mother, "eat your mush, and you'll be ready for anything."

Honu grabbed his bowl. "I think I better stay inside today." He shoveled mush into his mouth as fast as he could.

Grandmother, Mother, and Aunt Laura exploded into laughter.

The next morning was sunny, warmer than it had been for several months.

"There will be a Buffalo Dance on Second Mesa," Grandfather announced to Hester and Honu. "Your older brother, William, has been asked to dance."

"Why a Buffalo Dance?" Honu asked. "Buffaloes around here are only in school books."

"Once many lived to the north of us," said Grandfather. "Although we never hunted them, we know they are powerful animals. They carry away sickness and bring snow so our corn will have water in the springtime."

"I saw a Buffalo Dance last year," Hester announced. "People danced, not Kachinas."

"That's right," said Father, rising from the table. "It's a social dance." He tied a red band around his head. "Now, both of you go get ready."

"Hooray!" shouted Honu. He rolled up his sheepskin bed. "At last I get to see a dance."

"William's going to be a buffalo," Hester shouted. She ran to fill a pan with water so she could wash her hair.

"Two pickup trucks will carry people from our village," said Grandfather: "One for women and girls, and one for men and boys. I'll meet you outside."

A few minutes after Grandfather left, Aunt Laura walked through the doorway. "I heard about William," she said and clapped her hands.

"Yes," said Hester with a big smile. "He's going to be in the Buffalo Dance."

"That's not what I meant."

Hester looked from Mother to Father and back to Mother again.

Mother pressed her lips together. "Soon William will move away from us. He's going to be married and live with his wife's family."

"He can't go," Hester said, close to tears. "I'll miss him. Besides, who will bring home bundles of wood for our fire? Who will hunt rabbits for our stew? Who will help Father take care of the crops and herd the sheep?"

"I will," Honu said solemnly.

"You?" Hester's eyes widened.

Honu puffed out his chest and raised his chin. "I shall do William's work." He marched from the house, hoping this meant he was a man, even though he didn't want to be a husband.

In the village, sunlight poured unseasonable warmth on the bare arms of the women spectators. They had gathered to one side of the plaza. Some chatted with relatives and friends. The old ones sat on metal chairs and dozed. In the shadows on the opposite side of the plaza, stood the men, nodding greetings to each other, exchanging news. On the side streets, children dashed about. Among them two dogs jumped and barked.

Sharp drumbeats outside the village turned everyone silent. Hester and her friends stopped their game of tag and listened. A faint jingle of bells, a chant, scattered shouts, and the continued drumbeat. The sounds drew closer. Murmurs of "they're coming, they're coming," rose from the children.

They rushed back to the plaza, Hester and the other girls to the side with the women, Honu and the rest of the boys to the side with the men.

Two buffalo boys with shaggy heads, white-striped bodies, and black faces entered the square with bounding steps, bells jangling from a string at their waists. They stooped and alternately thrust to the ground the lightning stick in the left hand then the rattle in the right.

Behind them shuffled two buffalo girls in embroidered shawls and white boots, faces and hands painted white. They carried notched dance wands, moving them up and down to the drumbeat. Attached to their backs were large sun discs encircled by feathers.

The drummer came after the four dancers. And then fifteen singers entered the plaza with slow but sprightly steps. They sang a marching song interspersed with shouts and yelps, several waving bows and arrows. One of the singers fired a gun into the air. The procession stopped on the south side of the plaza. Grouping around the drummer, the singers began the song for the Buffalo Dance.

Hester carefully watched the girls dance forward in a reserved shuffle. One day she, too, would do this dance. She wanted to remember all the steps.

The girls shuffled around the back of the singers then down the center of the plaza. The buffalo boys bounded after them. Then the girls faced south, and the buffaloes sprang in front and danced out in a wide arc. The girls turned east. Again the buffaloes jumped in front and danced out. Then north, then west, in the same pattern.

They do this four times, Hester remembered. In her mind she saw herself performing the dance.

Now the buffaloes passed between the girls and each girl followed one, then the girls passed between the buffaloes and each buffalo followed a girl. Back and forth between each other, over and over, the girls with their shuffle step, the buffaloes stooping and leaping.

Buffalo Social Dancers
3rd Mesa

At one point the buffaloes pantomimed being wounded by the girls' sticks. They staggered and collapsed as if dead. Soon they leaped up, reborn, dancing energetically as before.

"*E-ya-he-na-yo-wi-na,*" slowly chanted the chorus again and again. And then faster, "*He-ya-a, he-ya-a....*"

When the dance was over, the drummer and singers marched from the plaza, leading the dancers who still kept the rhythm.

Not until they had disappeared did Hester think about William. She had watched the girl dancers so closely, she had forgotten to notice if William was one of the buffaloes.

"Was he there?" she asked Grandmother.

Grandmother shrugged and closed her eyes.

"It doesn't matter," Mother said. "The important thing is they danced well. Now visit your friends for a while. In about an hour another group will dance."

A large cloud in the shape of a Kachina inched up in the northern sky. Although Hester was aware of it being there, she didn't look at it. Nobody looked at it or said a word about its appearance. Instead, Hester knew her people were making silent prayers for snow. It was left to the voices of the singers, the beat of the drum, and the feet of the dancers to carry their prayers to the sky.

TIME: FEBRUARY, DURING POWAMUYA, WHEN LIFE IS PURIFIED.

# A VISIT FROM TWO KACHINAS

From outside came the sounds of a high-pitched whistle and a piercing cry. "*Hu-hu-huhuhu.*"

Hester and Honu rushed to the front door and opened it to see what had made the sounds. Mother and Father came over to join them. There stood a smiling Kachina with a white face.

"It's the Kachina Mother," Hester said breathlessly, backing away, "*Hahai-i Wuhti.*" She recognized the Kachina because her face was like the flat doll, the one tied by a string to the rafter. It had been Hester's first gift from the Home-Coming Kachinas when she was a baby.

*Hahai-i Wuhti* remained in the doorway, her hands hidden beneath her shawl. She looked extremely happy—round, red cheeks, smiling mouth, bright eyes peering through a red fringe. Her hair was long and black, and the small feather on top of her head fluttered in the wind as if alive.

"In four days," the Kachina cried in a high, squeaky voice, "the *Nataskas* will come. They may try to take away your children."

Mother said, "But the ogres only take away bad children. Our children are good."

Hahai-i Wuhti
infant doll

Hahai-i
Wuhti

"The ogres will decide that," said the Kachina. She held out an ear of corn. "Give this sweet corn to your daughter. Tell her to grind it. When the *Nataskas* come, they may take cornmeal instead of her."

Hester clutched Mother's skirt and hid her face in the folds, one eye peeping out.

*Hahai-i Wuhti* disappeared.

Immediately another Kachina, wearing old clothes—a patched pair of pants and shoes that didn't match—jumped into the doorway. His head was black, three white bars on each cheek, another three bars on his forehead. White-ringed eyes and a white-ringed mouth stuck out like thick antennae. Across the back of his head were shocks of brown hair.

"Who are you?" Father asked.

"Who are you?" echoed the Kachina.

Father scratched his head.

The Kachina scratched his head.

Honu and Hester laughed.

The Kachina laughed.

"You must be Mocking Kachina," said Father.

"You must be Mocking Kachina," was the reply

The Kachina thrust a group of tiny horsehair snares into Father's hands. "Tell your son to catch deer with these traps. The *Nataskas* may take meat instead of him."

Honu said bravely, "I haven't done anything wrong."

"I haven't done anything wrong," repeated the Kachina, and, as if by magic, he disappeared. Father closed the door.

Hester ran to kneel at the stone *metate* in the corner. She cut the kernels from the cob. Working as fast as her trembling hands would allow, she used the *mano* to grind the corn against the *metate*. Although she couldn't remember anything she had done wrong, she wasn't going to take any chances.

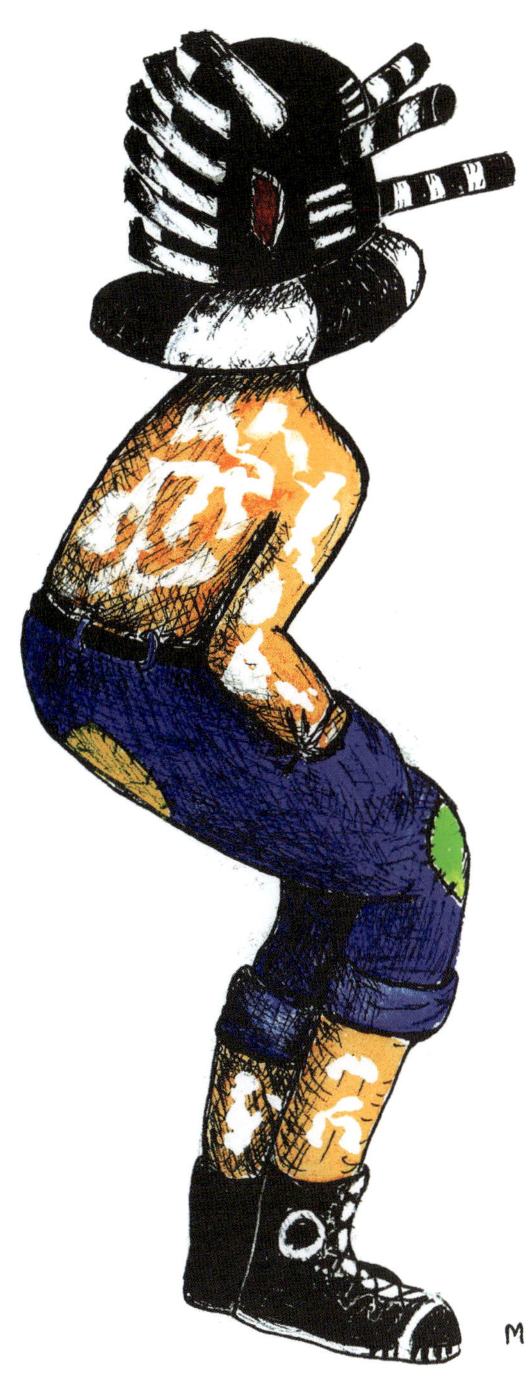

Mocking Kachina

Mother said, "That small bit of cornmeal won't be nearly enough to satisfy the *Nataskas.* I'll go into the storeroom and bring you a basket full of corn."

"A basket full?" Hester said in dismay, thinking her arms would fall off if she had to grind that much.

"Even one basket might not be enough. But you have four days. If you cannot do by yourself, I suppose I will have to help you."

"I can do it," Hester said with determination.

Honu went back to playing with his top, pulling the string so it spun around and around. He felt sorry for his sister having to work so hard.

In a solemn voice, Father said to Honu, "These horsehair traps are too small to catch a deer. You could, however, catch mice. I think that might please the *Nataskas.*"

"I don't want to catch mice," said Honu. "I'd rather spin my top."

For a while the only sounds heard in the house came from corn grinding and top whirring.

Then, Honu stole a look at Father whose face appeared serious. He looked sideways at Mother, who frowned back at him. At Grandmother, who sat by the window, her mouth turned down.

"The ogres won't bother me," Honu said in a small voice.

"I hope they won't," Father said.

"We would miss you," Mother added.

Grandmother coughed and stared out the window.

Honu began to wonder what the *Nataskas* considered bad in a boy. He remembered the time he hid behind the outhouse when Father wanted him to weed the corn, but how could the Kachinas know about that? And what about the time he played Eagle Kachina? And the time

William discovered him sleeping instead of herding the sheep? And the time....

Honu no longer enjoyed spinning his top. He stood up and attempted to sound casual. "Guess I'll try to catch a couple of mice in the storeroom."

Mother and Father nodded. Grandmother grunted, and the corners of her mouth turned up.

TIME: FEBRUARY, DURING POWAMUYA, WHEN LIFE IS PURIFIED.

# OGRE WOMAN

Four days later, before anyone else in the house was awake, Honu wrapped his black and white blanket around him and slipped outside. He had heard Mother say that all night Ogre Woman would dance below the mesa. Honu had never seen her. He wanted to sneak a look, although he knew what he was doing was wrong.

Shivering in the icy cold darkness, he stole away from his house. Nobody was around. When he reached the edge of the mesa, faint sounds of bells and chanting drifted up on the still air. Far below, close to the foot of the mesa, a fire burned as small as an ember. Across the light passed a spidery figure. A few moments later it crossed the fire again.

Was it Ogre Woman?

He held his breath, thinking if he breathed it might let whoever was down there know he was up here, watching. But he couldn't hold the air forever. Besides, he decided as he let air escape gradually from his lungs, she was down at the foot of the mesa, too far away to harm him. He would watch her for just a few minutes and then hurry back home.

When he had left the house, no one had been awake. Carefully he stepped over Hester and Mother, who slept on their sheepskins near him.

He tiptoed past Grandfather and Grandmother, whose snores sounded like a conversation in another language. Father and William hadn't been there, having spent the night in the *kiva*. Honu was glad, since they were light sleepers and probably wouldn't have liked what he was doing.

As he stood on the edge of the mesa, he remembered what Mother had said last night before they went to bed: "The old one will dance and sing around the fire. With the first sign of dawn she will walk up the path and pass through the village."

"Tell me about her," Honu had begged.

"Her name is Soyok Wuhti—Ogre Woman. She carries a bloody knife in one hand, a crook in the other. With her crook she reaches out to catch people. You wouldn't want to meet her."

Hester gasped. "Will she come in here?"

"No," Mother replied gently. "Soyok Wuhti never goes into houses."

"She wouldn't scare me anyway," Honu said.

Mother frowned. "You shouldn't say that. Now go to sleep. Remember what happens in the morning?"

"The Kachinas will bring presents," cried Honu.

"Yes, but only to children who have been good."

Now Honu shivered on the edge of the mesa and blinked at the dancing figure below, wishing for the eyes of an owl.

He wondered how long he had stood there. Had he been hypnotized by the speck of fire? By the faint jingle and the chant?

The eastern sky grayed. He continued to stare, no longer aware of how cold it was, forgetting he had intended only to steal a look and then hurry back to his warm bed.

A gust of wind brought back his senses. The fire below had died and the dancing figure was gone. Then, just under the ledge, a black cape whipped past. Jingling bells grew louder, mingled with clacking shells. He heard the slow tap, tap, tap of wood striking stone. With increasing dread

Honu realized someone was coming up the path. He wanted to run away but he couldn't move.

A shriek shot across the village. A chilling voice wailed, *"Soyoko-u-u-u, hoot, hoot, hoot."*

A dog barked. Another dog and another until every dog in the village joined the chorus.

Again, the wail tore through the air. Louder and louder grew the jingling, the clacking, the striking of wood against stone.

Over the edge of the mesa rose a frightful figure in a black dress and cape. She stood ten feet away from Honu. Her mouth was full of teeth. A long, red tongue hung down to her chest. Wild, gray hair flew around her huge head.

Honu stood rooted, paralyzed, terrified. "Soyok Wuhti," he breathed and thought he might never breathe again. She hadn't seen him yet. Maybe she would go the other way. Or, if she came this way, she might ignore him. If only he could disappear.

Her enormous head turned toward him. Slowly, from beneath her black cape, she withdrew an arm covered with blood. A knife glistened in her hand. She jerked up her other arm. The curved end of a crook shot towards him.

At that moment mother called, "Come home, come home."

Honu fled, his heart beating faster than the feet of a side corn dancer. Into the house he burst, shutting the door behind him. He dove under his sheepskin.

Grandfather sat up. "Honu, is that you? Is something wrong?"

Honu peeked out, wary as a mouse. "I heard Mother call," he gasped.

"Call?" crackled Grandmother, peering over at Mother, who appeared to be asleep. "Nobody here called you. Maybe you had a bad dream."

"I heard her," Honu insisted, rubbing his eyes.

"A good thing," Grandfather said knowingly.

Ogre Woman

With his blanket pulled tightly around him and warmth spreading though his body, Honu began to relax. He was safe. Ogre Woman wouldn't come into the house.

It may have been a dream, he thought. Perhaps I didn't leave the house.

An hour later, a Mudhead Clown came to the front door. When Hester opened it, the Clown, making funny noises, peered inside. He gave her a *tihu*, a small bundle of bean sprouts tied to it. Hester remembered that years ago, the same Clown had given her an infant *tihu*, the first kachina doll she had ever received. The Mudhead looked at Honu, made more funny noises and dashed away. During the morning two more Kachinas came to the house with gifts for Hester. They gave nothing to Honu.

Mudhead
Clown

TIME: FEBRUARY, DURING POWAMUYA, WHEN LIFE IS PURIFIED.

# NATASKAS

Mid morning an awful racket started up outside the house. Hooting and hollering, grunting and growling, stamping and rattling.

"What is it?" whispered Hester, looking fearfully at Honu.

"I don't know," he answered in a shaky voice.

The sound of a loud scrape came from the outside wall

Mother threw up her hands.

Father ran to the window. "It's the *Nataskas*," he shouted.

Mother said, "And to think last week I worked so hard plastering the outside wall."

"The ogres are trying to tell us something," Father said.

"Where's Honu?" inquired Grandmother, her voice rasping like insect wings.

Mother looked around the room. "He's disappeared."

'I'm hiding." Honu was hunched down behind the stove.

Mother said, "We better see what's going on outside."

Hester clutched Mother's skirt, trying to hold her back from the front door.

"Let go, Hester." Cautiously, Mother opened the door half way. A red-tongued Kachina stood outside. She wore a black dress and cape, and she carried a bloody knife and a crook with bells on it.

"*Soyok Wuhti*," Mother cried, "Ogre Woman."

Hester screamed. Honu groaned and hunched lower.

Behind Ogre Woman stood terrible-looking Ogre Maiden, a burden basket on her back. Even more frightening were the other three ogres. They had enormous black snouts, jagged teeth, curved horns, huge, popping eyes, and tall feather headdresses. They joggled toward the house, scraped the walls with shiny metal saws, and then joggled back. *Clop, clop, clop, clop, scr-a-pe, clop, clop, clop, clop....* Back and forth, back and forth.

Two *Heheya Kachinas*, one on either side of the ogres, whirled lassoes as if preparing to catch someone. They wore sheepskin tunics, their mouths were crooked-shaped and they had lightning stripes on their cheeks.

"Why are you here?" Mother called out the doorway.

*Soyok Wuhti* shrieked, "Your children are naughty."

Black Ogre

Heheya
3rd Mesa

"Not often," said Mother. "They are good children."

*Clop, clop, clop, clop, scr-a-pe, clop, clop, clop, clop....*

"We know what Hester has done," cried *Soyok Wuhti.* "Yesterday she laughed at Honu's new haircut. Last week she forgot to bring water up from the spring."

"I'm sorry," Hester said tearfully. "I'll never do those things again."

"Come live with us," Ogre Woman wailed.

Mother whispered to Hester, "Bring a bowl of your cornmeal. That's right. Give it to me." Mother held the bowl out through the narrow opening. "Here, Hester ground this sweet corn as a gift for you."

The *Heheyas* rushed up. Each poked a finger into the cornmeal as if to taste it. They carried the bowl over to Ogre Maiden, who shifted her burden basket, shook her head, and whistled in disapproval. *Soyok Wuhti* wailed, "Not enough. Not enough. Give us your daughter. We will teach her how to be good."

"Quick," Mother said to Hester, "bring the other two bowls. Careful, you're spilling the cornmeal."

Mother held the bowls out. "My daughter is a hard worker. She's a great help to me. Without her, my life would be much harder. Please don't take her away. Take her gift of cornmeal instead."

The *Heheyas* and Ogre Maiden examined the bowls. They squeaked and grunted as if they were having a conference. Meanwhile, the ogres with the black snouts continued to joggle back and forth, scraping the walls with their gleaming saws. Finally, the *Heheyas* gave the bowls of cornmeal to two Kachinas who appeared as helpers to carry away gifts.

*Soyok Wuhti* said, "We accept Hester's gifts. She may stay. We know she will continue to help you." Ogre Woman paused and then shrieked, "But we want Honu."

Father rushed over to the doorway. Mother backed away, pulling Hester along with her.

"Honu has done many bad things," wailed *Soyok Wuhti.* "Too many to list. Honu knows them all. He knows."

Father said, "Now, wait a minute. Our son means well. He just gets a little mixed up sometimes."

"He must get unmixed," screamed Ogre Woman. The *Heheyas* whirled their lassoes until they sounded like thunder, and the black-snouted ogres scraped harder against the walls.

"Honu is an excellent hunter," Father pleaded. "He can run long distances. And he tries to be brave."

"Give us Honu," wailed Ogre Woman. "We will teach him how to be good."

*Clop, clop, clop, clop, scr-a-pe, clop, clop, clop, clop....*

Father shouted, "Honu, bring those mice you caught. Hurry!"

Honu scrambled from hiding, dazed, forgetting where he'd left the stick on which he'd strung the four mice he had caught.

"It's under the table," rasped Grandmother.

Father gingerly handed the stick of mice out the doorway.

Hoots and howls followed and then a shrill whistle.

"Not enough. Not enough," cried Ogre Woman.

*Clop, clop, clop, clop, scr-a-pe, clop, clop, clop, clop....*

"Were those the only mice you caught?" Father asked Honu.

Honu nodded, trying hard not to cry.

Father looked at Mother. "What shall we do?"

"Give them the leg of lamb I planned to have for dinner," she answered with a look of resignation.

Father passed the lamb out the doorway.

"Not enough, not enough."

"Give them the *piki* bread and the squash," Mother said.

"They can have my top," screamed Honu, "and my bow and arrow."

"They don't want those things," said Father.

Mother wrung her hands as if in desperation.

"Forgive me," Honu said to his family in a trembling voice. "I'm sorry for the bad things I've done." He sniffed and wiped his eyes. "I've caused too much trouble. I'll go live with the ogres and learn how to be good." Setting his shoulders back as bravely as he could, Honu threw the door open wide. To his surprise, not an ogre was in sight

TIME: FEBRUARY, AT THE END OF POWAMU, IN THE YEAR OF PACHAVU, PLANT-LIFE-CARRIED-ON-PLAQUE.

# THE GREAT PROCESSION

Bearded Kachinas with horns on their heads raced through the village in the afternoon, waving yucca whips and hooting and stamping as if they were angry. The Whipper Kachinas soundly thrashed anyone foolish enough to remain outside. Mother covered the window with a blanket and told the children that *Hu Kachinas*, Whippers, roamed the streets. They are chasing off anything bad. "Stay away from the front door and window," she insisted.

When the hooting ceased, she said, "All right, it is safe to0 go now. This morning Aunt Laura set our chairs on the edge of the plaza, so we have a good place to watch the procession. Remember now, the chairs are for adults. You sit on the ground like the rest of the children. And Hester don't forget your shawl."

They joined the other families heading for the plaza. The day was gray, the sky heavy with clouds. An icy wind nipped their faces, tore at their clothing, sent tin cans clinking down the street.

Soon after they were seated, the Kachinas came, marching in from the south, each uttering a special cry. They followed the *Powamu* Chief and *Eototo*, the Kachina Chief, in a long line.

Behind the two Chief Kachinas came four Bean Maidens, carrying basketry plaques full of tall, brilliant green, bean sprouts. Helper Kachinas assisted the Maidens whenever their burdens grew too heavy, and Guard Kachinas protected the Maidens from any approach.

"What tall bean sprouts!" Hester exclaimed.

Honu nodded. "Where did they come from? Beans can't grow in our fields this time of year. It's too cold."

Mother leaned down. "The Kachinas brought them from their fields in the mountains."

Hester looked up at Mother. "My gift yesterday had bean sprouts tied to it. Did they come from the Kachina fields too?"

"Of course. Those are the ones we ate in the stew."

"But my doll only had a handful, and our kettle was full. Where did you get the rest of them?"

"Magic," muttered Grandmother, wrapping her shawl tighter around her.

Mother said, "The sprouts multiplied in the kettle. Now be still and watch what's happening here."

Many kinds of Kachinas paraded by. One had a pointed, blue-green head, another had flower ears. Many had feathers on their heads; some had beaks; and others had tube-like mouths. There were eyes that were round, sticking out like knobs, and eyes shaped like pothooks. Many Kachinas wore ceremonial kilts, although a number wore animal skins. Upper bodies, legs, and arms were painted, mostly in a similar design of red, yellow, turquoise, and white. Bells jingled. Turtle shells clopped. Weird calls and songs echoed against the stone buildings.

Eototo

On and on came the Kachinas, slowly, in all shapes, their colors brightening the dark afternoon, their warmth pushing the icy weather away. They had come to help the people start their growing season.

Mother touched Honu's shoulder as Badger Kachina passed, and Honu remembered it was Badger who had given him a bow and arrow last year.

"And there's Eagle Kachina," Honu whispered, wondering if the Kachina was still upset that he had tried to imitate him. "And there's Wolf and Antelope and a Whipper and...." His eyes widened as a handsome Kachina passed, a design of clouds on the cheeks, a fan of feathers atop the head. An identical Kachina followed. Each carried a spruce bough in one hand a bell in the other. They stood, singing, to the side of the procession. Honu poked Hester. "See them?" he said.

"Well, of course," Hester replied.

"Do you know their names?"

"Sh-h-h! We're supposed to be quiet."

"But I want to know."

"*Talavi*," Grandmother said, "Early Morning Kachinas."

Honu repeated the name softly, "*Talavi*."

When the Kachina Chief's Lieutenant moved past, Mother leaned down and said to Honu and Hester "That is *Aholi*."

"*Aholi*," they whispered, awed by the sight of the Kachina with the blue-green head and the colorful cape.

"I see Warrior Maiden," Hester said.

Mother nudged the children into silence.

Badger
Wolf
Antelope
Early Morning Kachina
Whipper
Bean Maiden

Aholi

Warrior Woman

Hester had heard about Warrior Maiden, who once lived in a red village far to the south. According to the story, one morning while she fixed her hair in the traditional butterfly whorls of a maiden, her village was attacked by enemies. Since the men had already left for the fields, the maiden grabbed a bow and a quiver of arrows and rushed out to protect her village. Because of her fierceness, the enemies fled. Because of her bravery, Warrior Woman became a Kachina. Always one side of her hair is long, for on that morning long ago she had no time to complete the other butterfly whorl.

More and more Kachinas arrived, so many Hester and Honu could not keep count. The Kachinas filled the plaza and moved around and around in a great circle.

The scene grew more complex—shapes, movements, joining together in a mass of swirling color. Songs, calls, clacks, jingles mingled and became one sound that grew in intensity and volume.

All at once, from somewhere in the plaza, a shout rang out.

The Kachinas froze—all movement ceased, no sounds. Absolute quiet reigned over the village. It was as if time had stopped.

A moment later the stillness was broken by the rustle of cloth as parents threw shawls over their children's heads.

Honu and Hester waited patiently, unable to see, knowing they shouldn't. Soon Mother pulled away the shawls as did all of the other parents.

The plaza was empty except for *Eototo* and *Aholi*, who slowly walked toward the street from which the procession had entered.

"Where did all the Kachinas go?" Honu asked.

"Into the sky, I think," said Mother.

Honu glanced up at the lowering, gray clouds but could see no trace of a Kachina.

Hester nudged him. "We're not supposed to look up there either."

With a nod of approval, Mother rose and folded her metal chair, leaning it against the wall. Grandmother struggled to her feet. The children scrambled up. All the spectators made preparations to go home.

It began to snow.

"The Kachinas are dancing in the clouds," said Hester.

Honu held out his hands, letting the snowflakes fall onto them. "They are sending presents to us."

Mother smiled. "Those are good thoughts."

Hester looked wistfully back at the empty plaza. "It was beautiful. I'll always remember how beautiful it was."

"Yes," agreed Mother. "Every four years it happens this way—so many coming."

"Then, next time," said Honu, raising his chin, "I'll be old enough to watch the Kachinas fly away."

Mother pursed her lips. "For now, you are old enough to help Aunt Laura carry the chairs back to her house."

TIME: FEBRUARY, FOLLOWING THE POWAMU CEREMONY.

# CLAN RACE

Father was the Racing Chief. He ran through the village early in the morning, bells and sheep hooves tied to his waist. At each *kiva,* he stopped to announce the coming kickball race, an event held as a prayer to the Kachinas for rain.

By noon the rooftops were crowded with people, and the barefoot racers began to gather at Flute Spring near the bottom of the mesa. It would be a clan race, twenty-four men taking part. All wore ceremonial kilts and had feathers tied in their hair.

Honu stood at the mesa edge with a group of older men and a few boys. He watched contestants file down the path. Looking out over the desert, he mentally traced the four and a half mile track the racers would cover. His brother, William, and Uncle Ramon passed by and started down. Father and Grandfather were already below to help start the race. A tingle of excitement rushed through Honu's body. He always felt like this before an important event.

Yesterday, on top of the mesa, there had been a race between village children. Honu came in third. He didn't care about not having won.

What bothered him was the knowledge that he could have done better. He hadn't practiced. Next year, he told himself, he'd be better prepared.

The racers below were lining up. Honu glanced up at the rooftop where Hester sat between Grandmother and Mother. He decided not to go up there and sit with them. Although the view would be better, he wanted to be closer to the race.

From the rooftop where Hester sat, dangling her legs over the edge, she couldn't tell who the contestants were. She could, however, make out the symbols they wore: yellow painted legs for Bear Clan; white stripe on the face for Badger; red disc for Sun; spots for Sweet Corn; green arm bands for Reed.

She said to Grandmother, "From up here, the racers look like rabbits."

Grandmother chuckled. "From down there," she said in her sandpaper voice, "we look like birds on a cliff."

Mother and Hester laughed as did the lady and the two boys who stood behind them.

"The racers have lined up," Hester said. "Why are they just standing there?"

Mother said, "The Running Chief is telling them to keep a happy heart so good will come from the race."

"The Running Chief is Father," Hester said proudly.

"It doesn't matter who the Running Chief is," said Mother. "The job is what is important."

A cheer rose from the spectators. The race had started.

Each clan had a ball, made of horsehair and pitch. The players drove the ball by cupping toes underneath and looping it forward. Other members of the clan ran ahead. When a ball landed, it was looped forward again. Across the desert they ran, kicking and racing westward from Flute Spring.

At the start Sun Clan led. Not far behind was Sweet Corn. The others were grouped in third place. Soon the racers disappeared into an arroyo. The spectators waited quietly for the runners to come back into sight after the southern turn.

"What is that little thing moving across the desert?" Hester asked.

Others had seen the same fast-moving figure and were asking each other what it was. Nobody knew except Grandmother, who sang out, "It's Warrior Mouse, trying to catch the big rabbits." The people on the roof laughed, although nobody understood what she meant.

The racers reappeared, moving eastward, then back toward the mesa in a wide arc. Closer and closer they came, kicking the ball forward.

"Sun still leads," cried a sharp-eyed boy.

The spectators grew more excited as the runners drew nearer. "Sweet Corn has caught up," someone shouted. The crowd cheered. "And here comes Warrior Field Mouse," screeched Grandmother. "Run, run." But nobody seemed to be listening to Grandmother. Their focus was on the clan racers. "Come on Sun." "Faster, Reed, faster." "Sun is ahead." "No, Badger is." "Sweet Corn is catching up." At the foot of the mesa, Badger took over the lead. All clans raced the last mile up the path to the mesa top.

The crowd scrambled off the rooftops and surged toward the finish line with shouts of "Badger, Badger, Badger."

The official announcement was made by Grandfather. Badger Clan had won; Sweet Corn was second. The contestants, breathing heavily, rested at the mesa edge before going to their *kivas*. Women returned home to prepare the feast for the racers, and Hester joined a group of children playing a game of tossing stones into squares drawn in the dirt. Only Father and Grandfather remained at the finish line, their eyes focused on the end of the steep path up the side of the mesa.

After a while, a small, weary boy staggered breathlessly to the top and crossed the finish line.

"Well, well," said Father, "an unofficial entrant in the race."

Honu nodded weakly and gasped, "I wanted to help."

Grandfather said, "The Cloud Spirits watched all who ran today. Soon they will send water racing across our land."

The next thing Honu knew, it was evening and Mother was kneeling beside his sheepskin bed, holding a bowl of stew.

"Here," she said, "eat this. You slept though the feast today."

From across the dim room Grandmother's voice crackled, "Eat and grow stronger, little Warrior Mouse. Soon you will catch the big rabbits."

TIME: LATE MAY, DURING HAKITONMUYA, TOO-COLD-TO-PLANT MOON.

# CORN DANCE

"I'm tired of this," Honu said to Hester, who was back from visiting a friend at the other end of the village. It was early morning, and he had been drawing in the dirt, but a mischievous wind kept creeping up and swirling away his picture.

Hester peered at it. "What are you trying to draw?"

"A buffalo."

She wrinkled her nose. "Looks more like a sheep."

He rubbed dust from his eyes. "It was a good buffalo. The wind took away the best part."

Another gust whipped up the ground. Hester covered her eyes and leaned against the house. Abruptly, she straightened up, uncovered her eyes and listened. "I hear the Kachinas!"

Voices and drumbeats rumbled like distant thunder. Rattles shook like summer rain against the corn stalks.

The house door opened and out came Grandmother, shoulders bent, eyes narrowed against the wind. She drew her shawl over her head and turned back to make certain the door was tightly closed.

"Bad weather," she muttered. "Bad for planting. Come along to the plaza. Your mother will join us later. She still fixes *piki* on trays."

Yesterday Hester had watched Mother make *piki* on the old, smooth stone Grandmother had found in her youth. As Mother dipped her hand into the thin, corn meal liquid and smoothed it over the hot stone, a fire beneath, Hester imitated, using a bowl of water and a small unheated stone of her own. Following Mother's movements, she pretended to lift the cooked, paper-thin *piki* and roll it up while it was still soft. After awhile, Mother let her work on the hot stone.

"We're making this food for the Kachinas," Mother had said.

Now, Grandmother led Hester and Honu along the narrow street, the sounds of drums, rattles, and chanting louder with each step. When they reached the plaza, Grandmother sat in a chair in front of Aunt Laura's house. She nodded greetings to the relatives on either side. Hester and Honu joined a cluster of children on the ground.

At the southwest end of the plaza, a group of Mudheads were chanting the song, one beating a drum. They wore a look of wonder—clay brown creatures with round eyes, round mouths and round knobs protruding from round heads. Five lines of Corn Kachinas, five Kachinas in each row, danced in the plaza in a stately manner, while beside them pranced two side-dancers, a thin veil of dust whirling around their bodies.

Periodically, a gust of wind blew up a curtain of fine particles that hid the chorus. The lines of Corn Kachinas moved slowly forward, right feet stamping hard with the added thrust of the right hand rattle, left feet echoing with the jingle of bells. The side dancers continued to prance and whirl up and down the rows, around and back, their feet scarcely touching the earth. Between gusts of wind, the sun shone brilliantly on their jewel-colored heads topped with feathers. *Stamp, jingle, stamp jingle*...they danced to the rhythm of the drumbeat and chant, their ceremonial sashes and painted bodies flashing.

Spotted Corn

Hester was amazed that the Spirits didn't seem bothered by the awful wind that kept whipping the sand about. Whenever the wind blew, she had to bury her face in her shawl and Honu hid his face behind her

That morning the Kachinas danced five times, a break between each set. Although the dances would last all day with rest periods between each set, most spectators would not stay to watch them all. Hester and Honu left with Grandmother after the first two sets.

In mid afternoon they returned to the plaza, Mother with them this time. The crowd was larger then. A dance set had just been completed, and the Spirits rested at the edge of the village.

A group of black-and-white-striped Hano Clowns, their horns topped with tufts of corn husks, appeared on two rooftops. They tumbled down ladders into the plaza and seemed startled to see the spectators. They ran about peering into people's faces with great curiosity.

A clown made a scary face at Honu and wiggled his fingers in a menacing way. Honu hid behind Mother's chair. Hester giggled and Grandmother cackled. Gathering courage, Honu peered out and made a face back at the clown, who fell over as if struck by lightning, bringing on everyone's laughter.

The clowns began to play leapfrog, leaping over any isolated person they could find. This brought more audience hilarity, especially when a clown jumped twice over an old, bent man, hunting for a place out of the sun. Even the old man seemed amused.

The clowns then lined up in the center of the plaza, arguing about who should stand where. They tied scarves between their horns and tried to perform a dance, but they couldn't seem to keep the rhythm. Not only was their dancing out of step, one clown danced in the wrong direction, and another jumped in the air until his scarf came loose and sailed into the face of another clown, who, unable to see, fell down.

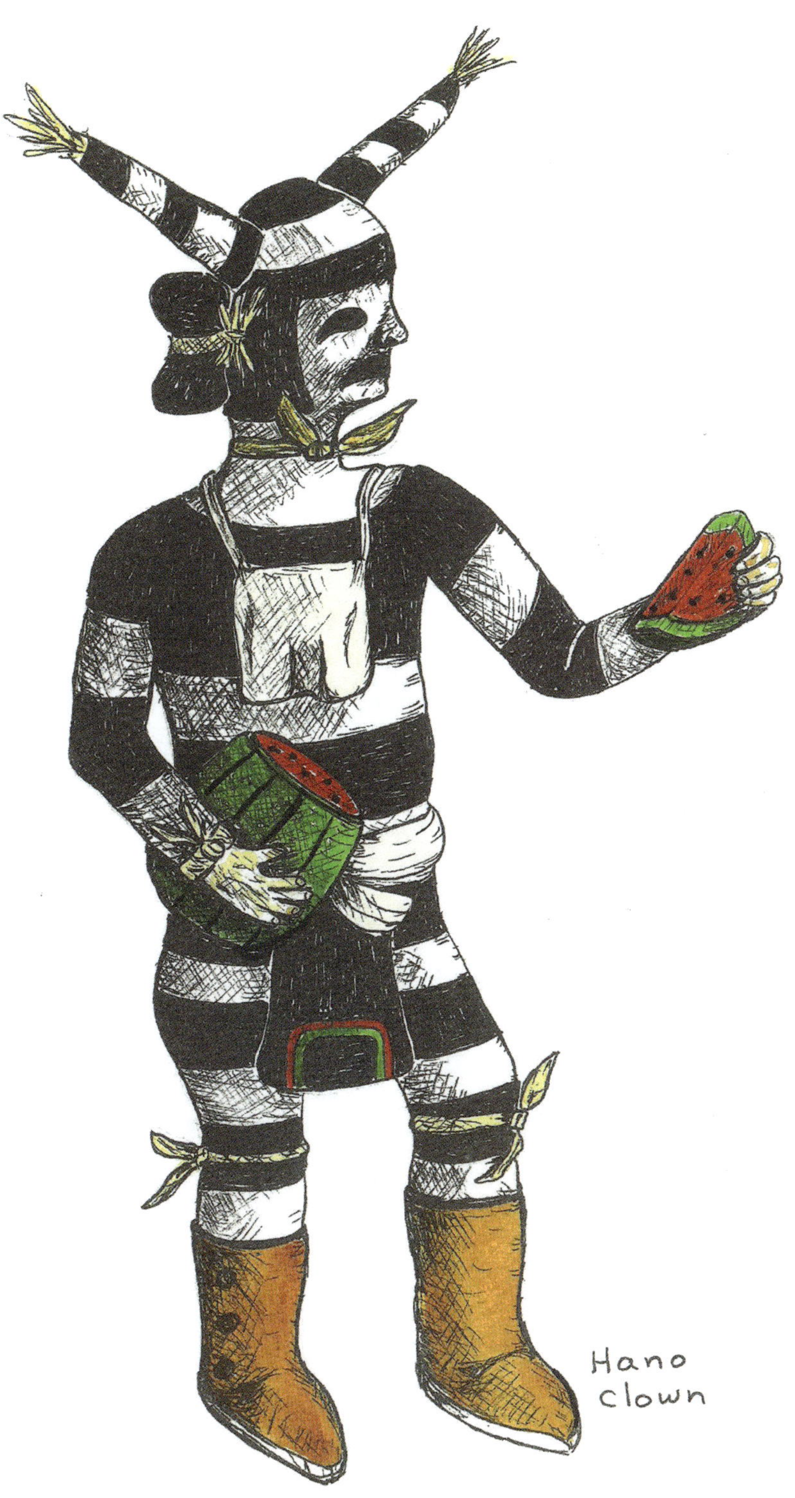
Hano
clown

Honu leaped to his feet and shouted, “You are worse than coyotes. You can’t dance at all.” Everyone burst into laughter, but Mother put her hand over Honu’s mouth, and Hester grabbed Honu’s arm and pulled him back down beside her. Muffled laughter and whispering continued all around.

An angry hoot silenced the crowd. It was Owl Kachina. He stood at the corner of the plaza, yucca whips in both hands, arms raised. He told the clowns they were acting naughty. They must stop this immediately.

The chief clown instructed his companions to find food before they got into any more trouble. The clowns ran around yelling for peaches and *piki,* which some women had brought, including Mother. While the clowns gobbled the food, they were fairly quiet. However, when they finished eating, once more they jumped around in a silly manner and made loud noises.

Honu glanced up at Mother. Her eyes told him to be still.

Again Owl hooted in anger and raised his whips. He chased the clowns from the plaza. The wind returned to annoy the spectators with stinging sand.

"Not a good sign," muttered Grandmother, shielding her face.

Three tourists arrived to watch the dance, but left when the dust storm concentrated on them. Shortly thereafter, the wind stopped blowing for the rest of the day.

Between dances the Hano Clowns returned to play jokes and games. Before one of the dance sets, the Corn Kachinas gave out gifts to the children, Hester receiving a *tihu* and Honu a miniature gourd rattle. At the conclusion of the ninth set, shortly before sundown, the Kachinas were led from the plaza for the last time.

Supper was late that night because Mother waited until Father came back from his duties in the *kiva*. As she dished up the bowls of lamb and hominy stew, Honu asked his Father, "How do the Corn Kachinas know when to visit us?"

"The men call up the Kachinas," Father replied in a solemn voice. "When we need prayers to be answered, we ask the Kachinas to come and carry them for us."

Honu sat still in a moment of awed silence.

A rap sounded on the door. Honu jumped, wondering if men had called up the Kachinas again. But it was his brother, William, returning home for a visit.

Hester showed him the *tihu* that a Kachina had given her that afternoon. "Look," she said, pointing to it, "white spots all over the body with holes in them. Don't they look like Mother's beads?"

"Your *tihu* is *Avachhoya*," William told her. "It is like the two Kachinas who were side dancers today."

"You saw the dance?" Honu asked in surprise.

"Yes."

"I didn't see you there."

"Well, I was," he said. "Now, look at the *tihu*, both of you. One of the ways you can tell a Corn Kachina is by the four horizontal feathers on the head. *Avachhoya* is the younger brother of *Hemis Kachina*. He always has these corn circles on his body and dances fast."

"It's a lovely *tihu*," said Hester.

"It appears to be carefully made," said William "I'm sure that the Kachina who gave it to you is happy you have it." He took a nail out of his pocket. Using a stick of wood by the stove as a hammer, he pounded the nail into a rafter alongside five other nails that held *tihus*. Carefully he looped the kachina doll's neck string over the nail.

"I got a gift, too," said Honu, showing William his rattle.

William nodded. "There's a story about its design. This round gourd stands for the earth, and the circle design on it is the sun. On each end of the earth sits a Hero Twin." He indicated the handle and the knob on the opposite side to which a feather was tied. "The Hero Twins keep our earth rotating so we have night and day. They send signals through the earth. That is the sound of the rattle."

Honu shook his rattle and listened. "What are the Hero Twins saying now?"

"They may be telling you to go to bed," answered Father with a slight smile.

That night a thunderstorm came to the mesa, clearing the dust from the air.

"Our prayers were heard," Grandmother said the next morning. "Our corn will grow."

TIME: JUNE, KELMUYA, THE PLANTING MOON.

# BUTTERFLY DANCE

"Is Hester here?" asked the young lady in the doorway. It was Paula from Mother's husband's clan. Behind her stood a ten-year-old boy—Ned, Paula's younger brother.

"Come in, both of you," said Mother. "Have some dried peaches. Hester isn't home from school yet."

Paula sat down at the table and took a peach. "We would like Hester to dance in the Butterfly Dance."

"But it's too early for the dance," said Mother. "Usually it's performed in August."

"I know, but my older sister and her husband are sponsoring one now because there has been so little rain for the newly planted crops. We hope the Butterfly Dance will help."

"I see." Mother stared thoughtfully out the doorway. "Hester is only nine, you know. She may be too young."

"I don't think so," said Paula. "And we need her. My little brother here thought it would be nice to dance with his pretty aunt."

Ned blushed and looked away.

Mother glanced out the doorway. "I see Hester coming now. Go ahead and ask her, Ned."

"I've been told," Ned said softly, "that the lady should ask the man."

Mother's eyes widened. "Hm-m-m, you're right. Well, then, go outside. I'll see what I can do."

Hester couldn't hold her excitement when she heard that Ned wanted her for a partner. She remembered seeing the Butterfly Dance last year. She knew that, like the Buffalo Dance, it didn't involve Kachinas.

"I'd love to be a butterfly with him," she cried and ran outside, calling, "Ned, I want to be your dancing partner." She peered around. "Ned? Is that you behind the storeroom? Why are you sitting on the ground back there? Are you hiding from me?"

"Of course not. I'm resting here to save my strength."

"Good. When do we start practicing the dance?"

"This evening, 7:00." He jumped up and ran down the street. "Don't be late," he shouted back.

Hester ran in the opposite direction to tell her friends.

"My goodness," Mother said from the doorway. "The butterflies have flown away."

Every evening for a week Hester practiced with Ned and the others until she knew the steps so perfectly she could do them without thinking, and once she dreamt she did. Even though no Kachinas were involved, she felt certain they would know if she didn't perform well.

The night before the dance, as was the tradition, Ned came over with her costume.

On the morning of the dance Mother sent for Thomas, her clan brother. Hester was already dressed in the woven black *manta* with a red, black and green design on her one-shouldered white vest. Thomas painted her feet with yellow clay and her cheeks with red. He put a silver and turquoise necklace around her neck. On her wrists he placed silver bracelets, and he gave her turquoise earrings to wear.

Mother brushed her long, black hair, scarcely dry from the dawn washing, until it shone. A fringe of horsehair was tied around her forehead so the hair fell over her eyes like a veil; colored yarn bands around her wrists and ankles; a maiden's shawl and bright kerchief around her shoulders.

Thomas set the large, brightly painted, wooden *tableta* on her head, tying the strings under her chin. He wrapped a braided lock of her hair around the strings in back to secure the headdress. Lastly, he rubbed sacred corn meal on her face. He stood back, gave her a final look over, then nodded to let her know he wished her well.

"Daughter," said Mother, "you are as lovely as the butterfly. Now dance with a happy heart."

First came the singers and the drummer, older men of the village, dressed in their finest clothes, Grandfather and Uncle Ramon included. They marched to the beat of the large kettle-shaped drum, filling the air with deep chanting that seemed to rise from the earth. Following them into the plaza were twenty-four dancers, who formed two lines, facing each other—a line of girls, a line of boys.

The girls were dressed alike, although they wore differently painted *tabletas*. In both hands they held spruce twigs. The boys wore black velvet shirts with multi-colored ribbons attached, ceremonial kilts, sashes, red moccasins, and capes. Two vertical red marks, the marks of the warrior, were drawn across their cheeks. They wore the tail of a fox to show their relationship to the animal world. Each boy carried a rattle and a spruce twig.

Hester thought Ned looked handsome in his costume. She was thrilled to be his partner and to wear the *tableta* he had made. However, as she glanced at the large crowd that lined the plaza and spread across the rooftops, she felt her stomach jump.

What if my *tableta* falls off? she worried. Ned was looking at her. His eyes seemed to give approval. I must do well, she told herself. I will dance with a happy heart.

Butterfly
Dancers

The dance began. With slow shuffling steps the two lines approached each other, arms and hands swaying, the bells on the boys' knees jingling. They countermarched to the right, to the left, and then down the center of the plaza while the song called for rain and the drum thundered the rhythm. On they danced, not a beat missed, not a mistake made.

Following their performance, there was a spirited Paiute Dance. After that, a group of young men and women in their late teens did the Butterfly Dance. In the afternoon all of the dances were repeated. A few of the aunts in the audience joined in the Butterfly Dance, pretending jealousy of their nephew's interest in his dancing partner. The villagers enjoyed watching the performers so much they asked them to come back the next day, which they agreed to do.

The evening was still warm. Hester climbed the ladder to the roof and lay watching the sky turn dark, waiting for stars to appear. She was tired but happy. For two days she had danced as a butterfly. Her happiness was not because of her success, although she knew she had done well, and it was not because she had looked beautiful, although she had appreciated the compliments. It was because she had been a part of something important shared with Ned.

"When I grow up," she whispered to the sky, "I may marry Ned." She smothered a giggle.

"Hello," said Honu. He peered at his sister from between the top two rungs of the ladder.

She sat up. "Did you like the Butterfly Dance, little brother?"

"Yes."

"Is that all you have to say?"

"No."

"Well?"

"Tomorrow I shall weed the melon patch, and in the afternoon I will herd the sheep."

"I'm surprised you want to work that hard."

He started back down the ladder. "And next year I, too, will dance," he said with determination just before he disappeared into the darkness.

Hester smiled, feeling quite grown up. "Next month I'll be ten," she announced to the sky and climbed down the ladder to help Mother fix supper.

TIME: MID JULY, DURING KYAMUYA, GO-HOME-KACHINA MOON, AT THE END OF THE NIMAN CEREMONY.

# THE KACHINAS GO HOME

Hester hugged her knees for warmth and listened for a sign that Grandmother was on her way down. She glanced at Mother, who sat at the table with a visiting relative. They, too, seemed to be listening.

Sometime in the hours before dawn, Grandmother had climbed the ladder to the roof and started her vigil as she did every year at this time during the *Niman* Ceremony.

The front door opened. Honu came in with an armful of juniper branches, and soon the fire in the stove snapped alive.

A cock crowed, followed by the sharp, shrill cry of a ceremonial eagle tethered on a nearby roof. Then footsteps sounded above.

Hester said, "Grandmother is coming down."

Mother nodded. "The Kachinas must be in the village. It's time to go to the plaza."

They left the house when the edge of the eastern sky began to lighten. Other families walked in the same direction, their footsteps like soft drumbeats. Children rubbed sleep from their eyes as they held to their mothers' or grandmothers' skirts. Older sisters carried babies. Members of a Hopi family living in Phoenix nodded greetings. They always came back for *Niman.* A few old men hobbled along with stoic determination.

A sudden breeze swept up from the desert below the mesa, fluttering women's shawls with the sound of bird wings. As if in answer, a burro brayed and a few dogs barked. The breeze disappeared. Once again the only sounds were footsteps.

After the villagers reached the plaza, they gathered around it and sat or stood quietly waiting. Three eagles on three rooftops also waited. Captured weeks before, they had been fed and tended with care, in preparation for their final sacrifice to the sky, a necessary part of the *Niman* ritual.

It grew so still Hester thought she would be able to hear a beetle move, if one crawled into the plaza. Then came rustling sounds like wind passing through a forest.

The Kachina Father and his assistant led thirty-six *Hemis Kachinas* into the square. On their heads were tall *tabletas* similar to those the Butterfly Girls had worn, terrace-shaped to suggest clouds. These were painted with symbols of germination and growth. The oblong eyes of the Kachinas and the narrow row of white circles down the center of their faces gave them an air of mystery. A ruff of rain-bringing spruce boughs, brought from the mountains, encircled their necks. More boughs hung down from their sashes. Many carried long, green stalks, ripe with corn, small toys and *tihus* attached; others carried melons, squash, bread—various foodstuffs. They stacked all in the center of the plaza.

Following the *Hemis* came eight *Manas* in white capes and white boots, hair worn in traditional maiden whorls. Each carried a large gourd, a wooden rasp, and a bone from the shoulder of a deer.

Hemis Kachina
Hemis Mana

A sense of peace flooded over Hester. She remembered feeling this way last year, and the year before, and for as many years back as she could remember, each time she sat with her family and watched the *Niman Kachinas* come into the plaza. Looking around at the villagers, many with their eyes closed, somehow she knew they all felt as she did.

The Kachina Father directed the *Hemis,* now holding only their gourd rattles, into a semicircle; the *Manas* with their instruments stood on the inside. A rattle shook—a signal for the dance to start. A few Kachinas stamped with their right feet and echoed with their left feet, then more Kachinas joined, then all, right feet stamping, left feet echoing, turtle shells clopping behind knees, rattles sounding a gentle *tush, tush.* The deep, guttural chant grew stronger.

Then the Kachina at the front of the line reversed direction. The next Kachina did the same, and the next. One by one they turned—a wave sweeping on down to the end of the line, turning like the seasons of life, one depending upon the other.

Grandmother, carrying a small pouch of corn pollen, rose and moved toward the Kachinas, as did a number of other ladies. They walked silently along the outside and then along the inside of the Kachina line, sprinkling corn pollen, blessing the Spirits.

Hester kept her eyes on Grandmother until she came back. Then she watched the *Manas,* knowing that as soon as the ladies finished blessing, they would kneel and play their instruments. The scrape of bone against rasp held over the opening of a hollowed gourd reminded her of the sound of frogs. Individual croaks came at first, then joined by all in a rhythm with the *Hemis,* who now faced the *Manas* and chanted and stamped with more vigor.

The Kachinas danced eight sets that day, remaining outside the village between each one. During the final set, late in the afternoon, the women who had been married that year came forward. Hester craned her neck to see if William's bride was among them. Yes, there she was in her white wedding robe like the others. She, too, carried a long bundle made of willow rods, her wedding sash inside, the fringe falling like rain from one end.

Before the Kachina Father led the *Hemis* into place for their last dance, the Spirits handed out more gifts—the last of what they had given several times during the day from the central pile: miniature bows and arrows and other toys for the boys; *tihus* for the brides and girls; food for the adults.

While the final dance was performed, Hester held her *tihu* carefully, for it was fragile—a *Hemis* with a delicately carved *tableta.* Beside her, Honu held his bow and arrow against his chest, his eyes focused on the Kachinas' feet.

Hester closed her eyes and listened. It was as if she stood in the center of the world and had become part of the pulse of life. "Bless you, Kachinas," she whispered. "Bring us rain."

It was sundown. The Kachina Father led the Spirits to the path at the edge of the mesa. Women came forward and took pieces of spruce from their costumes to plant in their fields for luck. Then the Spirits filed down the path to the desert below and disappeared.

Hester and Honu knew where they had gone. They had heard how after *Niman* the Kachinas traveled west to their mountain homes. There they would stay until next winter, when a few would start back to the villages, and gradually more would follow, returning to help the people. Each year they would come back, as long as the ritual was right and the belief was true.

On the following day the *kivas* were ceremonially closed for the season.

The next evening, it rained.

THE END

# GLOSSARY

*anai*—word for ouch.

arroyo—a dry stream bed.

bandolier—a broad belt worn over the shoulder.

bullroarer—a rectangular slat of wood on the end of a thong, which, when whirled makes a sound related to wind, thunder, and lightening. Usually a sacred instrument.

butterfly whorls—a traditional hairstyle for unmarried Hopi women in which each hair is drawn to each side of the head and fixed into a butterfly shape.

ceremonial sash—worn by men in ceremonies, woven of white cotton with embroidered ends in symbolic designs of red, green, and black wool.

ceremonial kilt—a short skirt worn by men in ceremonies woven of white cotton with symbolic designs embroidered on one end in red, green, and black.

clan—an association of families under one leader, having a common ancestor.

cornmeal path—a sprinkling of sacred cornmeal to indicate a way for the Spirits to travel.

Crier Chief—a designated man who climbs on his roof to announce important news to the village.

dance wand (a kind of prayer stick)—flat sticks cut and painted in symbolic designs with feathers attached, carried by certain dancers, used in ceremonies.

gourd—a squash-like melon which can be dried and used as a container or a musical instrument.

*haliksai*—"Listen, this is the way it is." A traditional opening for a story.

hatchway—a rectangular opening. To the Hopi, it indicates the entrance to a *kiva.*

Kachina (*Katsina)*—a messenger spirit or life force.

kachina (*katsina*) doll—see *tihu.*

Kachina (*Katsina*) Father—priest who has the honor of taking care of Kachinas while they are in the village, such as leading them in, assisting them in the dance, and leading them out.

Kachina (*Katsina*) Society—an organization with beliefs about Kachinas as Spirit helpers.

*kiva*—underground ceremonial chamber entered by a ladder. Sometimes there is also a side entrance.

lightning sticks—dance wand in the shape of lightning, carried by some dancers; also, another name for a bullroarer.

*mano*—stone used to grind grain, such as corn.

*manta*—traditional blanket-like, black dress, worn with one shoulder uncovered by Hopi women; also, a blanket-like cape.

mesa—a flat-topped mountain.

*metate*—a flat or hollowed stone on which grain, such as corn, is ground.

*pahos*—prayer feathers or prayer sticks; sacred sticks with feathers attached or feathers with cotton string attached in a special manner, used to send prayers.

*piki*—a tissue-paper-thin, cornmeal pancake, rolled up right after cooking, while still soft, often called *piki* bread.

planting the *pahos*—setting the sacred sticks or feathers into the ground to send prayers.

plaque—flat, woven basket.

plaza—square or court in front of the *kiva*; an area used for dances and other ceremonies.

prayer feathers; prayer sticks—see *pahos.*

quiver—holder for arrows.

rabbit stick—curved stick similar to a boomerang used in hunting rabbits.

rasp—a notched stick used as a musical instrument, when scraped makes a grating sound.

shrine—a sacred place where ritual acts are performed.

side dancer—dancer who dances outside the line of dancers.

social dance—a non-religious dance.

solstice—the northern hemisphere summer solstice (June 21), occurs when the sun is farthest north (the longest day); the northern hemisphere, winter solstice (December 21), occurs when the sun is farthest south (shortest day).

*tableta*—flat, wooden headd ress worn like a tiara by certain dancers.

*tihu*—kachina doll, made of dead cottonwood root and created to look like a Kachina.

yucca suds—soap made from the root of the yucca plant.

# KACHINA IMAGES IN BOOK

(Hopi names in italics, followed by page numbers of images)

Antelope (*Chop*), 57.
Badger (*Honani*), 57.
Bean Maiden (*Pachavuin Mana*), 57.
Black Ogre (*Nataska*), 47.
Eagle *(Kwahu*), 12.
Early Morning (*Talavi*), 57.
Hano Clown (*Koshari*), 71.
*Heheya* (no English translation), 48.
Home Kachina *(Hemis*), 85.
*Hototo* (no English translation), 9.
Kachina Chief *(Eototo*), 55.
Kachina Chief's Lieutenant *(Aholi*), cover, 58.
Kachina Mother *(Hahai-i Wuhti*), 32, 33.
*Kököle* (no English translation), 20.

Maiden (*Mana*), 85.
Mocking (*Kwikwilyaka*), 35.
Mudhead (*Koyemsi*), 44.
Ogre Woman (*Soyok Wuhti*), 42, 46.
Owl (*Mongwu*), 72.
*Soyal* (Solstice), 4.
Spotted Corn (*Avachhoya,* often a side dancer), 69, 74.
Warrior Maiden (*Hé-é-e*), 59.
Whipper (*Hu*), 57.
Wolf (*Kweo*), 57.

# NON-KACHINA IMAGES IN BOOK

Buffalo (*Mosairu*—social dancer), 29.
Butterfly (*Poli*—social dancer), 80.
Gift Rattle, 75.
Prayer Feathers (*Pahos*), 21.
Village with Kiva Hatchway and Entry Ladder, 2.
Warrior Field Mouse (*Tusan Tomich*—folklore hero), 15, 66.

# ACKNOWLEDGMENTS

Thanks to Barton Wright and the Lomayaktewa family for their help with the manuscript.

And thanks to Lynn Cooper, who meticulously painted my ink-drawn figures modeled from the kachina dolls in our collection.

Made in the USA
Charleston, SC
13 November 2014